SCHOLASTIC

Let's Find Out
My REBUS Reader

I0890040

I See Numbers

by Joan Michael

SCHOLASTIC INC.
New York Toronto London Auckland Sydney New Delhi Hong Kong

I see numbers on a  .

house

I see numbers on a  .

clock

I see numbers on a  .

shirt

I see numbers on a  .

train

I see numbers in my  .

soup

I see numbers on a  .

candy machine

I see numbers all around!